WALKS FOR ALL AGES
KENT

WALKS FOR ALL AGES

KENT

Hugh Taylor & Moira McCrossan

BRADWELL
BOOKS

Published by Bradwell Books
9 Orgreave Close Sheffield S13 9NP
Email: books@bradwellbooks.co.uk

1st Edition

Reprinted August 2017

ISBN: 9781910551417

Print: Gomer Press, Llandysul, Ceredigion SA44 4JL

Design by: Andrew Caffrey. **Typesetting by:** Mark Titterton

Photograph: Photographs © Hugh Taylor and Moira McCrossan

Front cover image ©National Trust Images/Nelly Boyd
Other images are credited separately.

Maps: Contain Ordnance Survey data
© Crown copyright and database right 2016

Ordnance Survey licence number 100039353

The information in this book has been produced in good faith and is intended as a general guide. Although the maps in this book are based on original Ordnance Survey mapping, walkers are always advised to use a detailed OS map. Look in 'The Basics' section for recommendations for the most suitable map for each of the walks.

Bradwell Books and the authors have made all reasonable efforts to ensure that the details are correct at the time of publication. Bradwell Books and the authors cannot accept responsibility for any changes that have taken place subsequent to the book being published.

It is the responsibility of individuals undertaking any of the walks listed in this book to exercise due care and consideration for their own health and wellbeing and that of others in their party. The walks in this book are not especially strenuous, but individuals taking part should ensure they are fit and well before setting off.

A good pair of walking books is essential for these walks. It is advisable to take good-quality waterproofs, and if undertaking the walks during the winter, take plenty of warm clothing as well. Because the walks will take some time, it would be a good idea to take along some food and drink.

Enjoy walking. Enjoy Hampshire with Bradwell Books!

CONTENTS

INTRODUCTION

Kent is 'The Garden of England', a pleasant, fertile land of orchards and gardens. It was the cradle of Christianity in England and a coast that has been frequently threatened with invasion over the centuries. The White Cliffs of Dover represent home to English exiles, while its history is full of shipwrecks and ruthless smuggling gangs.

The Cinque Ports were once powerful communities bound to provide ships for the sovereign in return for taxation advantages. Often no longer on the sea, they are now picturesque and interesting places to visit. Smuggling was rife well into the 19th century, particularly on Romney Marsh where you will encounter the story of the fictional Dr Syn, while touring well-preserved medieval churches. Churches were often used for storing contraband and the smugglers used signal windows in church steeples, such as the one at Lamberhurst, to communicate with one another.

Proximity to the Continent made Kent a hotbed of smugglers, but also left it susceptible to invasion, first by Napoleon and later by Hitler. Neither succeeded; Napoleon was defeated in 1805 at Trafalgar and Hitler by the Royal Air Force in the Battle of Britain in 1940. The defences against Napoleon are still visible in the Martello Towers along the coast and the Royal Military Canal. Although most of the airfields that defended against Hitler have been built over, you can visit the memorial to the Battle of Britain personnel on the White Cliffs, near Capel-le-Ferne. The Battle of Britain Museum is at the former Hawkinge Airfield and you can visit the cemetery where the airmen were buried. You can walk the beach at Reculver where Professor Barnes Wallis tested his bouncing bomb prior to the Dambusters raid on Germany's Ruhr Valley and see one of his prototype bombs at the Spitfire Museum at Manston Airfield. You might even be lucky enough to hear the drone of a Rolls-Royce Merlin engine then spot a lone Spitfire in the air above you.

There's much more to Kent than war and mayhem, however. At Canterbury you can visit the site where St Augustine brought Christianity to England and Chaucer set his pilgrims to walk. In Rochester you can see buildings that inspired Charles Dickens, while at nearby Higham you can find his dream house and the inn where he dined. Back on the marsh at Cooling is the church, where he imagined Pip finding the graves of his parents and little brothers.

OLDBURY

WALK ON THE RAMPARTS OF AN IRON AGE FORT, FOLLOW AN ANCIENT ROAD AND ENJOY THE DELIGHTS OF WINDING PATHS THROUGH COPPICED WOODLAND.

The huge Iron Age fort at Oldbury, one of the largest in Britain, is now hard to see in its entirety as it is covered in woodland, but after walking along the delightful narrow woodland path that is the Toll, your route back is along the edge of the fort. The broad plateau around you gives you an idea of the size of this fort. Excavations have shown little sign of permanent occupation here, where normally an entire village would have subsisted within the ramparts. Despite its size, it seems to have been primarily a defensive military position. Excavations have uncovered piles of sling stones and evidence of burning, suggesting a battle when it was overrun by the Romans. You can still see the remains of the ditch and ramparts and the cuts in the ramparts at the entrances, but the distinctive shape of an Iron Age hill fort is difficult to see, mainly because of the woodland, but also because of its size and the fact that the land has eroded over the centuries, softening and lowering its profile.

After the Toll, as you take the Waggon Road, you are walking right across the middle of the fort and also following the ancient road from Seal to Ightham, where there was a major crossroads for travellers. On Hasted's map of 1798, the line of the A25 is shown as the new road, a turnpike built in the 1760s. Along the edge of the fort there are ancient Palaeolithic cave shelters, but they are not easily accessible. Neanderthal flint tools have been found, suggesting that 50,000 years ago Neanderthal people were sheltering here, living a classic hunter–gatherer existence.

N Chadwick

Much later people took control of the earth's resources by cultivating crops and trees for specific uses. The ancient skill of coppicing trees has been practised for thousands of years to maximise yields of wood. It has now been re-introduced to the forest here. Look for trees cut right down with new shoots growing from the roots. Not only does it produce more wood in the thicknesses required for fence posts or handles or whatever, but it rejuvenates the tree, prolonging its life almost indefinitely, and provides a perfect open habitat for wildflowers, insects and birds.

THE BASICS

Distance: 3½ miles / 5.6km

Gradient: Moderate

Severity: Moderate

Approx. time to walk: 1hr 40mins

Stiles: None

Map: OS Explorer 147 (Sevenoaks and Tonbridge)

Path description: Forest footpaths, muddy in sections requiring boots

Start point: Car park off Styants Bottom Road (GR TQ 578558)

Parking: Off Styants Bottom Road (near TN15 0HB)

Dog friendly: Yes

Toilets: None on the route

Nearest food: Various restaurants, pubs and cafes in Sevenoaks

OLDBURY WALK

1. From the interpretation board at the end of the car park turn left and head uphill on a way-marked path. Continue on this through woodland, passing another way-marker post with the number 1 on it, then keeping ahead at a post numbered 2, to reach a clearing in the woods.

2. Turn left here and follow the path to reach a junction with a bridleway. Turn left and head uphill to reach eventually a junction with the end of a lane. Turn right here and take the public footpath, which skirts round the Camping and Caravanning Club site.

3. When the path ends at a road, cross over and enter Styants Wood on the other side then turn left at the interpretation board.

4. Take the narrow path through the woods, turning right onto a bridleway at a way-marked junction. Then turn left and head up some steps at another way-marker post. This is the permissive footpath through The Toll.

5. Now keep on a pleasant way-marked trail, which goes to the end of these woods before curving to the right and then emerging from the woods onto a clear grassy area. Turn right onto a narrow but well-defined footpath, which follows the edge of the woods before re-entering woodland and turning left onto a footpath.

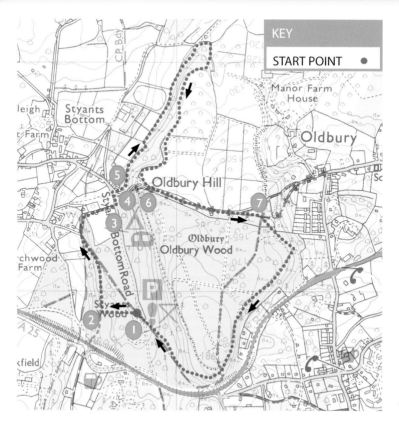

6. Then veer slightly right and downhill to join the Waggon Road, a muddy byway. Keep ahead at a way-marked junction and keep going to reach a four-way junction by another interpretation board. Keep ahead then bear right onto the right hand path signed 'byway'.

7. Again this is muddy in sections. This is the Eastern Ramparts of the Fort. Keep on this path, which will eventually come to a break on the ramparts. Head downhill on a steepish section then turn left to follow a broad footpath downhill. Near the bottom, when you can see the main road, bear right onto a narrower path and head into the woods. When the path forks keep right. At the next junction keep left and then when the path reaches the road, turn left to cross it and re-enter the car park.

LAMBERHURST

SMUGGLING, HOP AND GRAPE GROWING, A CRASHED WARTIME BOMBER AND FORMER PRIME MINISTER MARGARET THATCHER ALL FEATURE IN THIS WALK.

Lamberhurst is a pretty village in the Weald of Kent. It's an ancient settlement dating back to at least 1100 although a 1,500-year-old yew tree in the churchyard suggests an earlier settlement. The name means a wooded hill where lambs are found, and an early industry was wool production. In 1300, when a duty was levied on all exported wool, smuggling was rife. By the early 17th century this increased as exporting wool was declared illegal to protect the weaving industry.

Smugglers were called 'owlers' either because of the owl-like noises they used to communicate or because they worked at night. There's a window in the spire of St Mary's Church where owlers could light a lantern to signal to the next village that contraband was on its way. 'Brandy for the Parson and Baccy for the Clerk' ensured the compliance of the clergy. As well as taking wool to the Continent the smugglers brought in tea, brandy, tobacco and silk. In 1661 the death penalty was introduced to deter smugglers but this just resulted in them arming themselves to the teeth and becoming even more dangerous.

Almost three centuries later the danger came from the air, as the sky blazed with German bombers. On 24 February 1944 a German Heinkel 177 bomber crashed in flames on what is now the golf course and exploded on impact. There's a small memorial to Ernst Graff, aged 23, who died in the crash, just opposite the 11th tee on the walk route. The remains of the plane are still buried beneath the golf course. Denis Thatcher

played here, when he and his wife Margaret lived in Lamberhurst from 1965 to 1972. Denis had the reputation of being a prodigious drinker but he was not a beer drinker, which was unfortunate given that Lamberhurst was once a major hop-growing area.

The Kent–Sussex border ran through the village at one time. The price for Kent hops was much higher than for Sussex hops, so in 1894 part of the parish voted to join Kent. Now there is just one hop garden left at Lower Scotney Farm and the hops are used by Westerham Brewery to produce their Little Scotney Bitter. You will pass the remains of the hop-pickers; accommodation and cook house on the walk.

THE BASICS

Distance: 3½ miles / 5.6km
Gradient: Some moderate slopes
Severity: Moderate
Approx. time to walk: 2 hours
Stiles: None
Map: OS Explorer 136 (High Weald)
Path description: Grassy and muddy paths, metalled lanes and road
Start point: Chequers Inn car park (GR TQ 676361)
Parking: Chequers Inn, The Broadway (TN3 8DB)
Dog friendly: Yes
Toilets: At car park
Nearest food: Chequers Inn

LAMBERHURST WALK

1. From the car park go along past the pub and round into the pub garden. Go through the garden on the public footpath into playing fields. Head directly across the playing fields to a bridge into the golf course. Skirt the edge of the golf course to reach a gap in the hedge. Go through and across the grass to see the memorial to the German aviator. Return to the path and turn right.

2. Continue on the path ahead through the golf course, following the footpath signs to reach a gap in the hedge. Go ahead on a clear path through a crop field towards the road. Just before the road turn left down the side of the field and continue to a bridge.

3. Cross the bridge and with the river on your right go on to a fork in the path. Take the left path towards the church. At the church go left along the public footpath to exit the churchyard. However, you may want to spend some time exploring the church before you continue.

4. From the church gate go ahead on a gravel path, which continues onto a tarmac path and emerges at the road. Turn left down a path alongside the road as far as Brewer Street on the right.

5. Turn along Brewer Street and go on to the end, where it reaches a footpath sign and a gate into a wood. Go along this path as it moves in and out of woodland, eventually passing some old hop-pickers' huts on the right with a cook shed on the left. Shortly after that the path bends left and reaches a path junction.

6. Turn left here onto a lane, which soon becomes tarmac. Look for a footpath to the left. Go up some steps and follow the path through the vineyards until eventually you reach a road.

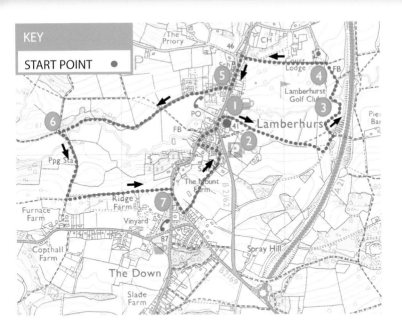

7. Go right and then bear left at the fork. Shortly after that, look for the stone marking the public footpath to the left. Go along here through a gate and follow the metalled path all the way past a school to a cul-de-sac of houses. Follow the road round to the main road and turn right and follow the road round back to the Chequers Inn.

SHIPBOURNE

Take a stroll on common land, see a revival of the ancient custom of carved signs and admire a 19th-century listed dog house.

Shipbourne Green, which is now a profusion of grasses and wild flowers, is where villagers once had the right to graze their animals. Just across the road from it is St Giles' Parish Church, an impressive Victorian building that replaced an earlier Georgian church that was beyond repair.

The highlight of this walk is Ightham Mote, a medieval manor house in the care of the National Trust. It was built around 1320 and a chapel was added in the 16th century. On the walk you see the outside of the house and while this is undoubtedly spectacular the real beauty lies within its courtyard. The seventy-plus rooms are all built around this. An unusual 19th-century addition was a dog kennel built for a St Bernard called Dido. It is the only Grade I listed dog house in the country.

During the late 19th century the then owner, Thomas Colyer-Fergusson, renovated the property, installed central heating and bathrooms and in the early 20th century opened it on one afternoon a week to the public. When he died in 1951 his son auctioned the contents and sold the house. Three local men bought it, then two years later sold it to a wealthy American, Charles Henry Robinson, who carried out further repairs and bought 17th-century English furniture for it. When he died in 1985 it was left to the National Trust.

There is a novel by Anya Seton, *Green Darkness*, which uses the building as a location and as part of the plot, as the skeleton of a female is found, walled up behind a blocked doorway. This was local lore but no evidence exists that a skeleton was ever actually found.

The last part of the walk is through the Fairlawne Estate, which belongs to well-known race horse breeder, Prince Khalid bin Abdullah Al Saud, the nephew of the first king of Saudi Arabia.

Towards the end of the walk you will pass the carved wooden village sign. Once such signs were commonplace but gradually they had all but died out. In 1924 King George VI made it known that he would like to see the old custom revived. Kent took up the challenge and now over half of its villages have carved or painted wooden signs.

THE BASICS

Distance: 3¼ miles / 5.2km

Gradient: A few moderate climbs and descents

Severity: Moderate

Approx. time to walk: 1½ hours

Stiles: Seven

Map: OS Explorer 147 (Sevenoaks and Tonbridge)

Path description: Field and woodland paths, some muddy and metalled lanes

Start point: Lay-by on Upper Green Road (GR TQ 593522)

Parking: Lay-by on common at Shipbourne (near TN11 9PE)

Dog friendly: Not really, some high stiles with no dog gap

Toilets: National Trust at Ightham Mote Car park

Nearest food: The Chaser Inn at Shipbourne, Café at Ightham Mote

SHIPBOURNE WALK

1. From the lay-by head towards the main road and the church. Go through the churchyard, passing to the right of the church. Exit the churchyard by a kissing gate and then immediately go right over a stile, with a yellow way-mark for the Greensand Way. You will follow these way-marks for the first part of the walk. Head across the field to the opposite corner to find a stile immediately followed by another.

2. Cross both of them and go along a footpath between two fences. When you reach a small clearing you will see another stile ahead. Cross the stile and take the footpath ahead alongside the woods. With the woods on your left, climb towards woods ahead. Keep ahead alongside the fence to enter the woods over a stile.

3. Follow the sometimes muddy path through the woods to a way-marked stile. Follow the path to a gap in the hedge and then go along the edge of a field with the hedge on your left to reach a gate and stile.

4. Go over the stile to the road and continue in the same direction along the road. When the road bends to the left, go through the gates to Ightham Mote. Follow the road round passing to the right of Ightham Mote. This is a National Trust property and well worth stopping to explore. You are now leaving the Greensand Way. Continue on the path; you will see blue bridleway markers now. The path winds along between hedges, passing a red way-marked footpath on the left, until it reaches a gate to the right.

5. Go through the gate and follow the path to the right to another gate and a left turn. Follow this broad muddy path to a road. Cross the road and enter the Fairlawne Estate. Follow the estate path around to the left, passing to the right of the house and turning right, following a footpath sign. Go through a blue way-marked gate and follow the clear path around the hill. Continue ahead to a crossroads of grassy paths.

6. Turn right towards the wood. Go straight ahead to go through a gate with the lake ahead of you. Go left along the estate road to a gate into a field and go along the edge with the hedge to your left. Cross a bridge into a crop field and take the broad path ahead through the field to a narrow gap in the hedge. This emerges

KEY

START POINT ●

onto a road with houses. Turn right, then left and then right and go ahead to the main road and the common. At the road, turn right along a grassy path beside the road and pass the carved wooden village sign to return to the start.

HIGHAM

Walk from Higham Station, where Charles Dickens would have caught the train to London, to his dream house at Gad's Hill Place, passing the church that he attended.

This walk underlines how much the countryside has changed in the 150 years since Dickens walked these paths. Starting at the station, Dickens would have been startled by the high-speed, smoke-free trains and the disembodied voice that tells you when the next one is due. One of the most unusual  pieces of freight to pass through here was a gift for Dickens from the actor Charles Fechter. It was a flat-packed Swiss chalet, which arrived in 58 boxes at Christmas 1864. It was erected in the garden of his house and he used it as a writing room. You can still see it at Rochester, where it has been rebuilt at Eastgate House.

The walk follows footpaths and roads that Dickens would have walked. However, the route would have looked significantly different to him on his frequent rambles in the countryside. The first part through a crop field was not cultivated then, but open countryside, but nevertheless he would recognise the panoramic sweep of the landscape. He would recognise too the country lane with White House Farm to the left. Although the rough lane would not have been tarmac, the ancient barn would have been a familiar sight. As he approached the main road, he would have walked by orchards, gardens and smallholdings, nothing like the massive fields we see today. Along the street to the church there were a handful of scattered houses and orchards.

The Church of St John was brand new for Dickens, built by his friend, the vicar, Joseph Hindle, in 1861, replacing the older church of St Mary because the centre of population had moved. However, no one at that time could have envisaged the growth of housing in the 20th century. Dickens would have walked the lane from the church to his house passing only orchards and gardens. Dickens's house, Gad's Hill Place, is now a school but you can see it from the road. The story goes that, as a boy, he often walked past here with his father and he loved this house. His father told him that if he worked hard he might one day have enough money to buy it and in 1856 he realised his childhood dream, bought it and lived there until he died in 1870.

THE BASICS

Distance: 4¼ miles / 6.8km

Gradient: Slight

Severity: Easy

Approx. time to walk: 1 hour 45 minutes

Stiles: None

Map: OS Explorer 163 (Gravesend and Rochester)

Path description: Footpaths, lanes and pavements

Start point: Higham railway station (GR TQ 715726)

Parking: Higham railway station (ME3 7JQ) (free)

Dog friendly: Yes (but keep on lead where indicated by signs)

Toilets: None on the route

Nearest food: Gardener's Arms and Sir John Falstaff, Higham (both on the route)

HIGHAM WALK

1. From the car park head to the station entrance then turn left and go back up the access road to the junction. Turn left into School Lane, then left again to cross the railway bridge in the direction of Cliffe Woods and Wainscott. At the end of the bridge pass Station House on your right then go ahead onto a footpath at a signpost and turn right.

2. Follow this narrow path beside crop fields until you reach a junction with a lane. Turn right and follow this past some converted oast houses on the right to reach White House Farm. Just past this the lane turns right.

3. There are two footpaths in front of you. Take the one on the right heading towards the church spire. When you reach the edge of the field, turn left and follow a footpath with a hedge on your right until you reach a junction with the road.

4. Turn right onto Hermitage Road and walk along it to reach the Church of St John. Enter the churchyard by a gate on the right and walk round it. Then explore inside. When you have finished exit the churchyard by the main gate and turn right again along Hermitage Road to a T-junction.

5. Turn left here, pass the Gardener's Arms and then the village library and keep ahead, down the hill until you reach the A226. Cross this carefully and turn left to reach the entrance gate to Gad's Hill School. It's private property so you can't enter but through the gate you can see the building that was once Dickens's home and where he wrote many of his most famous books. Continue for a short distance along the road before crossing back over to the Sir John Falstaff Inn where Dickens used to dine, then take the next right turn and head up Telegraph Hill.

6. At the junction turn right once more onto Hermitage Road and continue along it, passing the footpath on your left that you came from. After passing several houses look out on your left for a house called Medveza Gora and turn left after it onto a narrow footpath running downhill.

7. When you reach a junction turn left onto a broader footpath and follow it to the junction with White House Farm. From there retrace your outward journey back to the start.

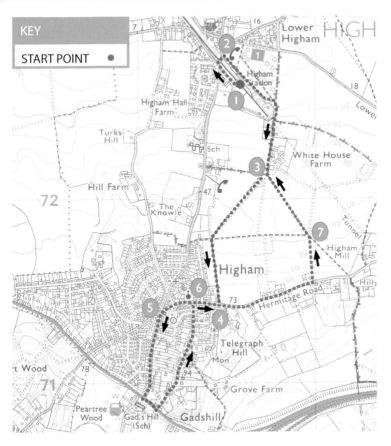

KEY

START POINT ●

CHARTWELL

The family home of Winston Spencer Churchill, Britain's great wartime leader.

Winston Churchill and his wife Clementine bought the house at Chartwell in 1922 and it was his main home until he died in 1965. The house itself was unimpressive but Churchill bought it for its view over the Weald of Kent. He spent the next two years having it transformed, extended and modernised. When work was completed it had five public rooms, nineteen bedrooms and eight bathrooms. Churchill also landscaped the grounds, creating a series of small lakes and a water garden where he kept fish.

Remuneration for politicians at that time was not great but he augmented this income with speaking engagements and writing. He was prolific and one of the best-paid writers of the time. He served as a newspaper war correspondent and columnist and wrote histories, biographies and even novels. But by 1938 his expensive lifestyle had led him to accumulate heavy debts and he decided to sell Chartwell. However, a financial rescue package offered by the industrialist Sir Henry Strakosch enabled him to keep the house and home that he loved.

In May 1940, on the resignation of Neville Chamberlain, he was appointed prime minister and led the country throughout World War II, boosting morale and determination with his oratory. Following the evacuation from Dunkirk and just before the start of the Battle of Britain he called on people to brace themselves and bear themselves so that if the Empire lasted for a thousand years it would be said that 'This was their finest hour.'

In August 1940, as the Battle of Britain was being fought in these very skies he famously declared that 'Never in the field of human conflict was so much owed by so many to so few.' By the end of October it was over and the 'Few' had put paid to Hitler's plans to invade Britain.

During the war the Churchills didn't use Chartwell because it was too close to the Channel and would have been vulnerable to air attack or a lightning ground raid. They returned after the war but the costs of running the property were beyond their means. Again it was wealthy businessmen who came to the rescue, buying the estate then renting it to them for a nominal amount for the remainder of their lives. When Churchill died in 1965, his widow gave it up and it was transferred to the ownership of the National Trust.

THE BASICS

Distance: 4 miles / 6km

Gradient: Many climbs and descents, some steep

Severity: Moderate

Approx. time to walk: 2 hours

Stiles: Three

Map: OS Explorer 147 (Sevenoaks and Tonbridge)

Path description: Woodland paths (some muddy) and country lanes

Start point: Car park at Chartwell (GR TQ 455515)

Parking: At Chartwell (TN16 1PS) (charge except for NT members)

Dog friendly: Yes, if they can manage stiles but on lead near livestock

Toilets: At Chartwell

Nearest food: Café at Chartwell

CHARTWELL WALK

1. From the car park head back to the road. Cross the road and take the footpath opposite, which is the Greensand Way. The first part of the walk follows way-markers for the Greensand Way. Continue ahead to a fork, where you go right. Go along this woodland path, keeping ahead and following way-markers to a T-junction at a fence. Turn right and continue to the road.

2. Cross the road and re-enter the woods, still following the Greensand Way way-markers. Fork to the right of April Cottage and then fork left. When you reach a crossroads with a bridle path turn left and follow a narrow path through the woods. This path gets very narrow and overgrown at times so if you want to avoid it continue on the Greensand Way to the next junction and turn left. Either way you arrive at a crossroads of paths.

3. If you took the first path you turn left, and if you took the second path you go straight ahead on the path down to the road. Cross the road and look for steps to your left. Go up here and turn immediately right to reach the memorial bench to Octavia Hill's mother. Beyond the bench go over a stile and cross a wildflower meadow to another stile, leading to the National Trust memorial (Octavia Hill was one of the founders of the Trust). Follow the path past the memorial and turn right down alongside a field, eventually reaching a road.

4. Turn right along the road, until at a bend just opposite an oast house, there is a public footpath sign to Crockham Hill Church. Follow this down steps, past some pretty gardens then along a boardwalk to a stile. Cross the stile to a wildflower meadow and follow the path to a bridge and a gate and across a field to another gate into a picnic area. From the gate turn right to the church to visit Octavia Hill's grave and the memorials in the church.

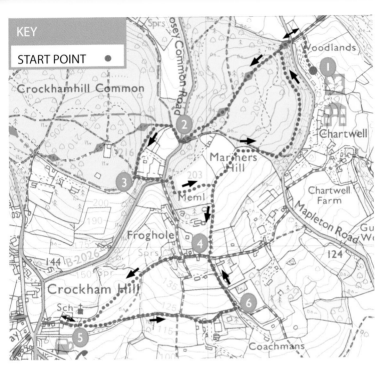

5. From the church go down the road past the school and look for some steps on the left. Go down the steps onto a grassy path and cross to a gate in the hedge. Go through onto a country lane and turn left along it until you reach T-junction.

6. Go left onto a path through the woods, which emerges onto a country lane and reaches the path you took from the National Trust Memorial. Return by this path, turning right at a T-junction, following the Octavia Hill Walk way-markers. Follow this path through the woods, looking out for Chartwell House across the road to your right. Eventually you will reach a T-junction with the Greensand Way. Turn right here and retrace your steps to the car park.

ROCHESTER

DISCOVER HOW CHARLES DICKENS LOVED THIS TOWN,
SPENT A LARGE PART OF HIS LIFE HERE AND IMMORTALISED IT
IN HIS NOVELS.

Dickens knew Rochester as a boy, when the family lived at Chatham and his father took him for long walks in the area. In 1856, he bought Gad's Hill Place at nearby Higham (see Walk 4). You can now see his Swiss chalet from the garden at Gad's Hill, in the grounds of Eastgate House in the High Street. Eastgate House was built in 1590 and provided the model for Westgate House in *The Pickwick Papers* and the Nuns' House in *The Mystery of Edwin Drood*. On the other side of the street a large 17th-century timber-framed house became Mr Pumblechook's premises in *Great Expectations*.

Just around the corner is one of the most atmospheric creations in Dickens's writing, Satis House in *Great Expectations*, based on Restoration House in Crow Lane: 'Miss Havisham's House … was of old brick, and dismal, and had a great many iron bars to it. Some of the windows had been walled up; of those that remained, all the lower were rustily barred. There was a courtyard in front, and that was barred.'

Inside, Pip found Miss Havisham, in the remnants of her once-white wedding clothes, the bridal table covered with spiders' webs and all the clocks stopped at the moment that she learned she had been jilted. The name of Restoration House is derived from the fact that Charles II stayed here on his way to London to be crowned.

Opposite Restoration House you go through the Vines, which was the monks' vineyard, to reach the cathedral. Founded in AD 604, the present building dates to the 11th century. *The Mystery of Edwin Drood*, Dickens's last and unfinished novel, centred on the idea that a mysterious corpse was hidden there. Dickens himself was almost buried there too. In his will he directed that he should be buried 'in an inexpensive, unostentatious and strictly private manner'. The family had planned a simple burial but acquiesced to an approach from Rochester Cathedral, where a vault was then prepared.

However, Rochester's vault was left empty when the Dean of Westminster Abbey requested that he should be laid to rest in Poets' Corner.

Opposite the cathedral, 12th-century Rochester Castle made Dickens think 'what a brief little practical joke I seemed to be, in comparison with its solidarity, stature, strength and length of life'.

THE BASICS

Distance: 2 miles / 5.6km
Gradient: Flat
Severity: Easy
Approx. time to walk: 1 hours
Stiles: none
Map: OS Explorer 163 (Gravesend and Rochester)
Path description: Pavements and lanes
Start point: Rochester Cathedral car park (GR TQ 743686)
Parking: Rochester Cathedral Car Park, Northgate (ME1 1LS) (charge)
Dog friendly: Yes, but keep on lead
Toilets: Castle Gardens, Castle Hill
Nearest food: The High Street has many cafes, restaurants and pubs

ROCHESTER WALK

1. Exit the car park and turn left into High Street. Pass the tourist information office on your left then look out for The Poor Travellers' House on the same side. On the next corner is La Providence. This French Hospital was founded, in London, by Huguenots 250 years ago. They took over these early 19th-century houses in 1960 as apartments for elderly people of Huguenot descent. Continuing along the High Street, pass Blue Boar Lane and Eastgate House and gardens, then cross the road to the 17th-century mansion which became Mr Pumblechook's house before turning back along the High Street the way you came.

2. Turn left into Crow Lane to reach Restoration House near the top on the left. Then enter the park called The Vines opposite the house and walk through it, keeping left at the junction to exit at the other side opposite the former Archdeaconry. The frontage is 18th century but the house behind it is much older. Turning right to go down this street you pass Oriel House on your right. Look for the two fire marks belonging to the companies that insured this 18th-century building against fire.

3. Take the first left into The Precinct then the next left to turn into St Margaret's Street. A short way along this, on your right, is the Coopers Arms, reputedly the oldest pub in Kent. Then turn back downhill and turn right, then veer slightly left to go through the 15th-century Prior's Gate. Turn right along Minor Canon Row, built in 1723 to house the lesser clergy. Number 7 was a later addition to provide a home for the organist. Look for the plaque on the wall of one of the houses. This was the childhood home of the actress Sybil Thorndike and her brother Russell, author of the Dr Syn novels, which you will encounter in the Old Romney walk (Walk 18). Head back the way you came to a T-junction with Boley Hill.

4. Turn right to visit the cathedral and when you are finished turn left and walk to the top of the street with the castle on your right. Look for a sign indicating the site of the original Roman South Gate on a house to your left.

5. Turn right into St Margaret's Street and follow the road round to the left and then turn right through a gate to enter the castle grounds. Veer left across the grounds,

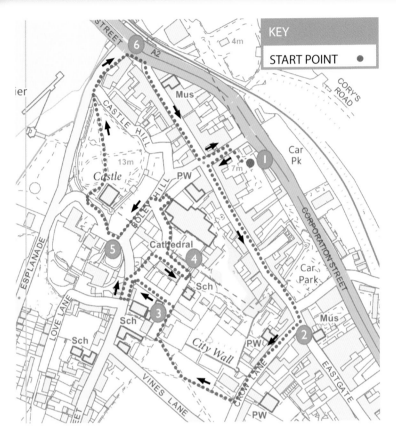

then go down some steps, through a gate and turn right onto the Esplanade. Along here on your right is the 14th-century Bridge Chapel, which is now a meeting room for the Bridge Trust.

6. At the junction turn right back into High Street and continue along it, passing the Guildhall (now a free museum) on your left and across from it the Royal Victoria and Bull Hotel. This is where a young Princess Victoria spent the night in 1836. On the left of the street is the early 18th-century Old Corn Exchange with its impressive clock. Opposite that is the King's Head Hotel. When you reach the 15th-century Chertsey's Gate on the right you are near the end of the walk but before that look on the left at Abdication House, which is now Lloyds Bank. James II of England and VII of Scotland spent his last night in England here before heading to exile in France. Then turn left down the narrow lane to return to the car park.

iStock

Rochester Cathedral

Rochester Castle

COOLING

GREAT EXPECTATIONS IN A COUNTRY CHURCHYARD AND LATER WITH JOOLS HOLLAND!

The opening paragraphs of Charles Dickens's novel **_Great Expectations_** are set in the churchyard of St James at Cooling. On a Christmas Eve, a seven-year-old orphan boy kneels in front of a grave in a forlorn and overgrown churchyard. In addition to the tombstone to his father and mother, whom he had never known, there were 'five little stone lozenges, each about a foot and a half long, which were arranged in a neat row beside their grave and were sacred to the memory of five little brothers of mine'.

Visit on a fine summer day and it is picturesque. But on a wintry afternoon, as the mist rolls in from the Thames estuary, the marshes beyond the church are desolate. Dickens used this setting to describe Pip's encounter with Abel Magwitch, an escaped convict, 'A fearful man, all in coarse grey, with a great iron on his leg. A man with no hat, and with broken shoes, and with an old rag tied around his head. A man who had been soaked in water, and smothered in mud, and lamed by stones… who limped and shivered, and glared and growled'. Magwitch terrified Pip into returning the next morning with food and a file; 'Or I'll have your heart and liver out.'

There has been a church here since the late 13th century. It is mainly constructed of ragstone and flint with the nave, chancel and lower half of the tower being part of the original building work and the remainder of the tower completed in the early 14th century.

Not much in the way of alteration then happened until the 19th century with the addition of a porch and the vestry and interior renovations like a new pulpit and stairs. Inside look out for the 500-year-old door opposite the current doorway. You can still open it but the north doorway is now blocked.

Although the church is no longer in use for regular worship it was the location, in 2005, for the marriage of musician Jools Holland to Christabel McEwen, daughter of Scottish artist and folk singer Rory McEwan. It was a star-studded guest list that included Stephen Fry, Ringo Starr, Robbie Coltrane and Dawn French. The Hollands have a home just along from the church, built inside the medieval ruins of Cooling Castle.

THE BASICS

Distance: 3½ miles / 5.6km
Gradient: Flat
Severity: Easy
Approx. time to walk: 1½ hours
Stiles: Two
Map: OS Explorer 163 (Gravesend and Rochester)
Path description: Country lanes and field footpaths
Start point: St James's Church, Cooling (GR TQ 756759)
Parking: Lay-by at St James' Church, Main Road (ME3 8DG)
Dog friendly: Yes
Toilets: In Cooling village near church
Nearest food: Pub in Cooling village

COOLING WALK

1. From the lay-by go around the church on the road to the left and then follow the road round to the right. Go along the road until you come to a fingerpost for Cooling Court and Spendiff and turn left.

2. Follow this pretty country lane past Cooling Court Farm and under the railway bridge to a right turn.

3. Turn here onto Cooling Street and continue to the next right turn at Spendiff. Go along another country lane and turn left and continue alongside the railway to a T-junction.

4. Turn right under the railway bridge and go ahead on a lane, looking out for the footpath at Gattons Farm.

5. Turn right through Gattons Farm and follow the footpath sign across a crop field to a stile. Cross the stile and go across the next field to cross another stile. Follow the path to the corner of the field and go through by the side of a broken stile into another field. Follow the line of the footpath to a hedge and then turn left along the hedge to reach the road.

6. At the road go straight ahead and then follow the road round to the right. Go along it, passing the gatehouse towers of Cooling Castle on the left. At the next tower look for the line of the castle moat, which can still be clearly seen. You will then be back at the junction where you turned left at point 1. So retrace your steps from here to the start.

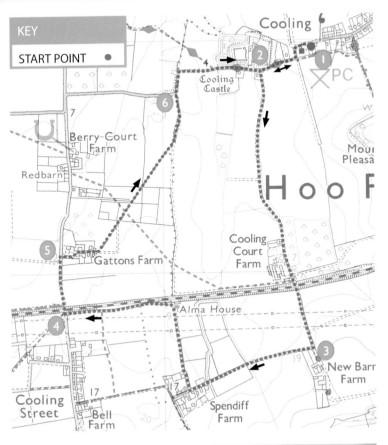

KEY

START POINT ●

Cooling

Cooling Castle

Berry Court Farm

Redbarn

Gattons Farm

Cooling Court Farm

Alma House

Cooling Street

Bell Farm

Spendiff Farm

New Barn Farm

Mount Pleasant

H o o

PC

CANTERBURY

Step into the past, as you follow in the footsteps of Queen Bertha of Kent through this World Heritage Site. Then walk around ancient city walls and admire architecture spanning more than a thousand years.

The World Heritage Site consists of Canterbury Cathedral, established around AD 600 by Augustine and rebuilt in the 11th century, St Augustine's Abbey and the church of St Martin, England's oldest active parish church.

St Augustine arrived in England in AD 597 on a mission from Pope Gregory to convert the Angles. He used the church of St Martin's, which had been renovated for Bertha, the wife of King Ethelbert, who was a Christian. Augustine founded the abbey and the cathedral, establishing Canterbury as the centre of Christianity in England. In the 10th century the cathedral became a community of Benedictine monks, which continued until Henry VIII dissolved the monasteries in 1540. Damaged over the centuries by the depredations of the Civil War, World War II and time, this magnificent building has seen countless alterations and additions but parts of the Norman building can still be seen.

The abbey was built to house Augustine and his monks but only a small part of the remains date from that time. It grew over the centuries into a massive community, with a huge church and burial places for kings and abbots. St Augustine was buried here and you can find the plaque which marks the spot beside one of the pillars.

You are following the route that Queen Bertha would have taken every day from the royal palace, close to where the cathedral is now, passing beyond the walls by the Queningate, to worship at St Martin's Church. Look for the bricks and tiles from the Roman church and for a blocked doorway, which may have been the entrance to Bertha's church before Augustine enlarged it. The tower is a 14th-century addition.

On the way back, look for the almshouses founded by John Smith in 1657 and the water pump provided by John Hales in 1733. Your path along the city walls passes the Dane John Gardens and mound, once a Roman cemetery, then a Norman castle and a public park since the late 18th century. Passing by quiet gardens and the river, along narrow lanes of historic buildings, by the end you will feel that you have scarcely scratched the surface of this fascinating city.

THE BASICS

Distance: 3½ miles / 5.6km
Gradient: Flat
Severity: Easy
Approx. time to walk: 2 hours
Stiles: None
Map: OS Explorer 150 (Canterbury and the Isle of Thanet)
Path description: Pavements, cobbled streets and city walls
Start point: Tourist Information Office, 18 High Street (CT1 2RA or GR TR 148578)
Parking: Park and Ride, New Dover Road (CT1 3EJ)
Dog friendly: Yes but keep on lead where appropriate
Toilets: Tourist Office and Castle Row on the walk
Nearest food: Many outlets in the High Street

1. With your back to the tourist office turn left and head along High Street. Take the second turning on the left into Mercery Lane and follow it towards Christ Church Gate to arrive in the Butter Market. If you want to visit the cathedral precincts you need to pay the admission fee at Christ Church Gate. It is expensive but it is an awe-inspiring building.

2. Turn right along Burgate passing on your right Butchery Lane, Longmarket, Iron Bar Lane, Canterbury Lane and finally arrive at Burgate Lane.

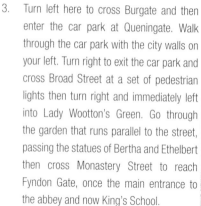

3. Turn left here to cross Burgate and then enter the car park at Queningate. Walk through the car park with the city walls on your left. Turn right to exit the car park and cross Broad Street at a set of pedestrian lights then turn right and immediately left into Lady Wootton's Green. Go through the garden that runs parallel to the street, passing the statues of Bertha and Ethelbert then cross Monastery Street to reach Fyndon Gate, once the main entrance to the abbey and now King's School.

4. Turn right along Monastery Street passing Church Street on your right before turning left into Longport. Look out for the water pump with a plaque relating to it on the wall. Keep on Longport to reach St Augustine's Abbey on your left. You will get a good view of this through the railings but the entire site is well worth a visit (there is an admission charge). When you are finished with the abbey

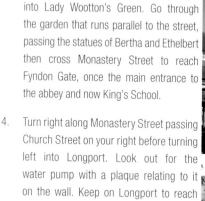

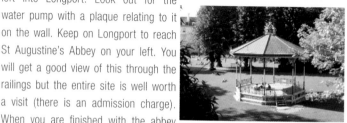

continue along Longport passing the 19th-century Old Session House and Prison on your left and shortly afterwards on your right the almshouses.

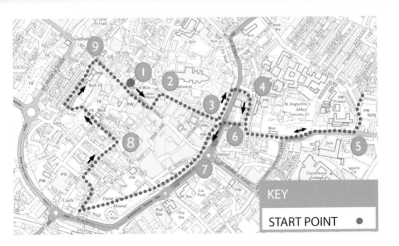

5.   Next turn left into North Holmes Road and head towards the Lychgate for St Martin's Church. The noticeboard gives details of the times it is open for visitors. Fans of Rupert Bear should make their way past the church and onto the terrace at the back. Turn left and along the back to seek out the grave of Mary Tourtel, the creator of Rupert. Then retrace your steps back to Monastery Street.

6.   Turn left into Church Street, cross Broad Street at the pedestrian lights and turn left into Burgate Lane. Head along here passing the Zoar Chapel to the junction with St George's Street. Cross the pedestrian crossings to head up onto the city walls.

7.   Follow the walls looking out for the 16th-century coach house, the Flying Horse, and the Dane John Gardens, exiting the wall towards Northgate. Turn right here and pass the public toilets to continue along Castle Row to reach the White Hart Inn. Enter a small garden area to the left of the inn and cross it on a path that exits onto a junction with St Mary's Street and Castle Street. Keep ahead along Castle Street passing Hospital Lane and Adelaide Place then turn left at the 15th-century Three Tuns Inn into Beer Cart Lane.

8.   At the T-junction cross Stour Street and bear slightly right to go along Water Lane, pass Canterbury Punting and cross a bridge over The Great Stour to continue on the Franciscan Way and over another bridge to enter Greyfriars Garden. Bear left on the path and exit the park through a gate. At the end of a short alley turn right into St Peter's Grove and follow it, keeping straight ahead when the road turns left, to continue on a narrow lane which ends at T-junction.

9.   Turn right into St Peter's Street, which continues as High Street to return to the start.

RECULVER

THIS STRETCH OF COASTLINE IS RICH IN HISTORY, FROM A
ROMAN FORT AND A SAXON CHURCH TO THE FINAL TESTS
OF PROFESSOR BARNES WALLIS'S FAMOUS BOUNCING BOMB.

During May of 1943 the coastline to the east of Reculver became the testing ground for the famous bouncing bomb invented by Professor Barnes Wallis. They were eventually used in Operation Chastise on the night of 16–17 May when Lancaster bombers from 617 Squadron dropped them on three massive dams in Germany's industrialised Ruhr valley. The Möhne and Edersee dams were breached, flooding the Ruhr and Eder valleys and killing 1,600 people. Despite the destruction of two power stations, several factories and mines, the Germans effected speedy repairs and production was resumed within four months. The bombs dropped on the Sorpe dam caused only minor damage.

What Wallis designed was essentially a depth charge. It was to be dropped in such a way that it would reach the dam then sink to the required depth before exploding. It was cylindrical in shape and was started spinning backwards before being dropped. This spin allowed it to bounce across the water much like skimming a stone. This meant it would clear the dam's defences. When it got to the wall the remaining spin helped hold it there as it sunk. But that was just part of the solution. It had to be dropped at the correct low altitude while the aircraft was flying at a designated speed.

A new squadron was formed to carry out the raid. In command was Wing Commander Guy Gibson, who had flown over 170 missions although he was just 24. They were based at RAF Scampton in Lincolnshire. The aircraft were modified to carry the bombs and had most of their armour removed to save weight. The correct altitude and the exact spot to release the bomb were calculated. Nineteen Lancasters took off on the raid, three had to turn back and eight were lost. Only eight made it back including the one piloted by Gibson. Fifty-three crew members were killed and three were taken prisoner.

Of the prototype bombs tested at Reculver, two lay embedded in marshland behind the sea wall until 1977, when the army recovered them. In 1997 several more were removed from the sands. You can see one of them in Herne Bay Museum and another at the Spitfire and Hurricane Memorial Museum on the Isle of Thanet.

THE BASICS

Distance: 4½ miles / 7.2km

Gradient: Flat

Severity: Moderate (easy, apart from the last section)

Approx. time to walk: 2 hours

Stiles: None

Map: OS Explorer 150 (Canterbury and the Isle of Thanet)

Path description: Hard-surfaced footpaths, farm track and narrow, overgrown footpath

Start point: Car Park at Reculver Country Park (GR TR 226692)

Parking: Reculver Country Park Visitor Centre (CT6 6SS) (charge)

Dog friendly: Yes

Toilets: At Visitor Centre

Nearest food: King Ethelbert Inn, near car park

RECULVER WALK

1. Exit the car park and bear left onto a footpath heading past the towers of the ruined medieval church. This was the site of the Roman fort of Regulbium, which was abandoned in AD 200 after two centuries of occupation. In the 7th century it became a Saxon monastery and later still the church of the monastery became the  local parish church until early in the 19th century. It was abandoned because of coastal erosion. The towers were saved from demolition because they were used as markers for coastal navigation. Be sure to stop and read the various interpretation boards and try to imagine what the Roman fort looked like.

2. When you reach a T-junction turn left onto the Wantsum Walk. The Wantsum was once a wide channel with the Isle of Thanet beyond it. The passage started to silt up by the 12th century, marshlands were formed and navigation was no longer possible. The marsh was drained to create farmland in the 17th century and today the Wantsum is a very small river that runs beside the next part of the walk.

3. Follow the path round to the right and then continue for a couple of miles along the coast. This is the area where the RAF conducted their final tests on the bouncing bombs prior to Operation Chastise. When they were being tested, their inventor, Barnes Wallis, would watch from the edge of the beach and then, as his son later revealed, 'I shall never forget the old man coming home and telling mother that he had taken his shoes and socks off, rolled his trousers up to the knees and waded into the water to see what happened to the bombs.'

4. When the path bears slightly right look out for a fingerpost to your right just before the path bears left again. Turn right onto a broad track and follow it until you reach a junction.

5. Turn right, then bear left on a narrower path up an embankment and then keep ahead on a long, straight, grassy track running parallel to a railway track. When this ends at another junction turn right and along another section of track with a tall banking to your left. Keep on this as it bends to the left and when it reaches another banking bear right and uphill on a narrow footpath.

6. You are now on the slowest part of the walk along the top of the Rushbourne Sea Wall. The path is firm but very narrow and in the summer can be rather overgrown. Shorts and short sleeves should be avoided; wear good shoes or boots and carry a walking pole to help bash through the worst of it. Eventually pass a fish farm on your right then follow the track round to the right and past a gate to turn left onto the outward route from where you can retrace your steps to the start.

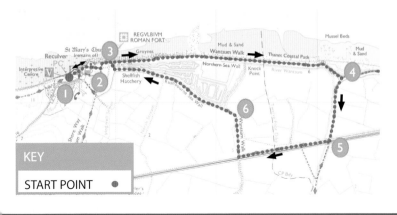

KEY

START POINT ●

DOVER

An unforgettable stroll along the White Cliffs of Dover, in sight of Dover Castle and the busy ferry port.

The iconic white cliffs were formed around 100 million years ago, from the remains of tiny sea creatures and plants. Over millions of years these calcified remains sank down to the bottom of the sea until eventually, as the seas receded, this layer of white chalk or limestone became part of the land. The cliffs stay white because of natural erosion. Chalk is soft and is eroded easily by wind and waves.

It is impossible to be unaware of the history as you walk here, looking for bluebirds, with that song running in your head. You are only 22 miles (35km) from France and the ferries shuttle back and forth constantly. Nowadays that is a benefit to the locals, as they can nip over to France for lunch or to stock up on cheese or wine. But in the dark days of World War II, the inhabitants of Kent expected to be the first to be invaded by the Germans and watched as British fighters fought off the superior forces of the German Luftwaffe in the skies above them. Although the threat of invasion was thwarted by the airmen of the Battle of Britain, the White Cliffs still formed the front line and gun batteries were constructed all the way along the coast. Long-range guns were installed to prevent German shipping using the Channel and they sank or damaged twenty-nine German ships over the period.

However, Hitler was by no means the first to attempt invasion here. The Romans succeeded in landing in Kent and Napoleon planned to invade but didn't, while William the Conqueror built a wooden stockade here after the Norman Invasion of 1066. There was probably an Iron Age fort on the spot and the lighthouse built by the Romans can still be seen. The medieval stone castle at the core of the present building was built in the 12th century by Henry II and has been added to over the centuries. Significantly, throughout that time this strategic point was continuously garrisoned right up to the 20th century.

Whether as an important defensive position or a sentimental image of home for English people abroad, there is no doubt that the White Cliffs are known the world over as an icon of England, as recognisable as the Houses of Parliament or a red London bus.

THE BASICS

Distance: 2½ miles / 4km

Gradient: Undulating

Severity: Moderate

Approx. time to walk: 1 hours

Stiles: None

Map: OS Explorer 138 (Dover, Folkestone and Hythe)

Path description: Well-surfaced footpaths

Start point: White Cliffs of Dover Visitor Centre (GR TR 335422)

Parking: At the visitor centre (CT16 1HJ) (charge)

Dog friendly: Yes but keep on lead where indicated by signs

Toilets: Visitor Centre

Nearest food: Visitor Centre

DOVER WALK

1. With the visitor centre behind you turn left onto a grassy path running beside the access road, then continue on a broad, well-surfaced footpath to go through a kissing gate. Bear left and take the path heading gently uphill. There are great views of Dover harbour on the right and, if you look backwards, Dover Castle. When you reach the end of this path go through a kissing gate and enjoy your first glimpse of the White Cliffs. Then head downhill on a narrow footpath to reach a junction with a kissing gate on your right.

2. Ignore this and instead turn left onto a path heading to Langdon's Hole. Go down some steps then bear left. After another set of steps keep left, ignoring further steps to your right, then head along a broader path heading gently uphill to reach a kissing gate.

3. Go through this and turn right into Harbour Field. This is where you must put your dog on a lead. Walk along the edge of the field with the fence on your right then go through another kissing gate and turn right onto a well-surfaced path. Keep on this to reach another kissing gate on your left and re-enter Harbour Field.

4. Walk along a grassy path with the fence on your left this time, Go through a kissing gate, then turn right.

5. This broad, grassy track now heads gently downhill back towards the port and the castle. Go through another kissing gate back into Langdon's Hole then keep ahead on a well-worn path going down some steps then up some others. Finally reach a set of steps on the right that you came down on the way out and turn left.

6. You are now on another broad path with cliffs on your right. Continue to go through a kissing gate then turn left to reach a viewpoint where you will have the

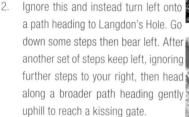

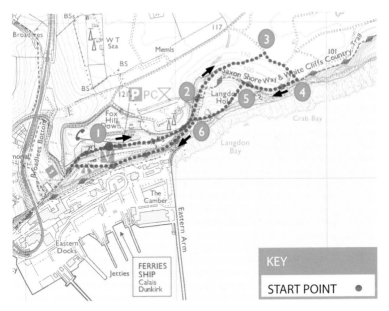

best view of the White Cliffs on this walk. When you are finished return to the path and keep ahead. When you see a narrow path branching off to the right go onto it and head steadily uphill. At the top when you reach a gate turn right and go up some rough steps to the picnic area, bear right across it then cross the road and take to footpath back to the visitor centre.

iStock

SANDWICH

A STROLL AROUND A MEDIEVAL TOWN, A WALK ALONG THE RIVER AND THERE MAY EVEN BE A LIVELY FAIR IN PROGRESS IN THE SQUARE.

Sandwich is an ancient port on the River Stour. It was one of the Cinque Ports, a confederation of ports along the south coast, established by Royal Carter in 1155. They had a duty to provide fifty-seven ships for fifteen days' service each year to the king. In return the ports enjoyed privileges, such as exemption from import duties, which inevitably led to their becoming centres for smuggling. The Cinque Ports gradually lost power and influence until by the 16th century their status had become almost entirely ceremonial. Several of them, like Sandwich, are no longer even on the sea.

The town still has many of its medieval buildings, testament to its former importance. All the way along Strand Street to the Quay, the street is lined with medieval timber-framed houses. There is the Pilgrim House, which consists of two merchants' houses, and the King's Lodging, built around 1400, where both Henry VIII and Elizabeth I were said to have stayed. When you arrive at the Quay, the Barbican is the 15th-century arch that all traffic had to pass through to cross by the ferry and later by the bridge, built in the 18th century. Look under the arch for the list of tolls being levied in 1905. The tolls continued until 1977. The swing bridge, which spans the river now, was opened in 1891. If you are lucky you may see it opening to let a boat through. On the right as you continue from the Quay, look out for the 14th-century Fisher Gate, the only medieval gate still surviving.

Later in the walk, as you go along the town walls, you can see the shape of the moat alongside. When you come to the part called the Ropewalk, it is filled with water. This section of the wall was used at one time for rope-making, so that they could stretch out long, straight lengths of rope.

The historic medieval centre of the town is at the square, which is dominated by the 16th-century Guildhall, with an oak-panelled courtroom and a council chamber where the town council still meets. This is also where you can find the Tourist Information Centre if you want to linger in this charming town.

THE BASICS

Distance: 4½ miles / 7.2km

Gradient: Flat

Severity: Easy

Approx. time to walk: 2½ hours

Stiles: None

Map: OS Explorer 150 (Canterbury and the Isle of Thanet)

Path description: Pavements, lanes and well-surfaced footpaths

Start point: Gazen Salts Car Park (GR TR 329585)

Parking: Gazen Salts Car Park (CT13 9EU) (charge but free on Sundays)

Dog friendly: Yes

Toilets: At the quay (charge)

Nearest food: Several cafes and restaurants in Sandwich Town centre, passed on the walk

SANDWICH WALK

1. Exit the car park onto Strand Street and turn left. Pass St Mary's Church then keep going to reach Breezy Corner, then pass the Pilgrim's House and King's Lodging and a little further on the Sandwich Weavers on the right. At the junction, with the Admiral Owen on your right and the Bell Hotel opposite, turn left, passing the Crispin Inn on your left and go through the arch of the Barbican towards the toll bridge.

2. Turn right just before the bridge and walk along the path beside the river, passing the public toilets on your left. At the end of the path, where it turns right towards a car park, bear slightly right to cross to a grassy area then keep left to follow a footpath by the riverside. Keep on this as it becomes a broad, well-surfaced, footpath.

3. When you come to a footbridge over the river turn left to cross it then take the footpath at the other side. At a T-junction turn left. At a junction of paths keep ahead on the Saxon Shore Way. This continues for some distance, going through woodland, across meadows and another footbridge before reaching a crossroads with a lane.

4. Turn right and follow the lane beside a golf course then turn right again onto a road at the next junction. Follow this road to the next junction then turn right again, over a bridge and keep on this road for about a mile back into Sandwich. Shortly after you pass the junction with St George's Road on your left, then the Tennis Club on your right, cross the road at a bridge and turn left onto the Mill Wall.

5. The walk now continues round the town walls, crossing Dover Road and continuing along the Rope Walk. When you reach Fellowship Walk on the right, turn right and walk along the side of the car park to reach the rear of the Guildhall. Keep to the right of the building and go through a narrow passage to enter the Cattle Market.

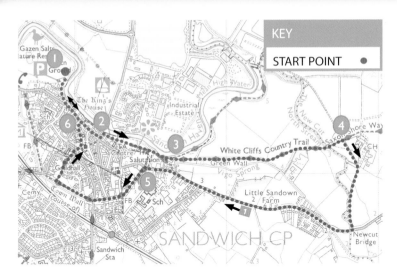

Turn right in front of The Market Inn and then first left into No Name Street. Bear left to cross Delft Street then turn left into Market Street. At the end of this keep left along The Butchery, then veer left across Harnet Street to arrive at Breezy Corner.

6. Turn left along Strand Street and return to the car park.

SANDWICH ROMANS

Take a pleasant walk by the River Stour to explore an ancient Roman fort.

When the Romans, under Emperor Claudius, launched an invasion of Britain in AD 43, they initially landed here at Richborough. Although landlocked now, Richborough then was a coastal location, with a natural harbour, on the Wantsum Channel. The initial invasion force created a defensive beachhead, which in time became a supply base and a couple of decades later had developed into the thriving maritime town of Rutupiae.

This was an important settlement and the gateway to Roman Britain. In the year 85 the Romans built one of the largest monumental arches in the entire Empire here, the site of which can be seen in the middle of the fort. By 277 it had become a shore fort surrounded by massive walls to protect Roman Britain from seaborne raids by Saxons and Franks. The Romans were here for a further 150 years before abandoning the site.

Watling Street was an ancient trackway that the Britons used to travel between St Albans and Canterbury. When the Romans took over they paved it and extended it so that it linked to Richborough, Dover and their other channel ports. You can still see in outline the second-century shops that ran along Watling Street. They were open at the front and had rooms behind them that were used for accommodation or storage. The outline of the bath house, in the north-east corner, are the highest standing remains.

The most obvious and impressive part of the remains are the late third-century defences, particularly the flint, stone and concrete core of the walls. When this was built it would have been faced with stone blocks and you can still see parts of that construction in the north-west corner. Outside of the walls the settlement was protected by two wide, deep ditches. Later, in the mid-third century, further ditches were created by digging through the shops and houses of the settlement to turn it into a military installation.

In the north-west corner are the remains of a Roman baptismal font, hexagonal in shape and made of tile. It's Christian and a very rare example of Christian remains from a time when Christianity first became legal. To the east is the medieval chapel of St Augustine, which was still in use as late as the 17th century.

THE BASICS

Distance: 3½ miles / 5.6km

Gradient: Mainly flat

Severity: Easy

Approx. time to walk: 1½ hours

Stiles: Two

Map: OS Explorer 150 (Canterbury and the Isle of Thanet)

Path description: Road, river path

Start point: Gazen Salts Car Park (GR TR 329585)

Parking: Gazen Salts Car Park (CT13 9EU) (charge but free on Sundays)

Dog friendly: Yes, if they can manage stiles

Toilets: At Roman Fort car park

Nearest food: Many pubs and tearooms in Sandwich

1. From the car park take the path at the end into the recreation ground. Pass to the right of the Cricket Club Pavilion and head for the path in the left-hand corner of the field. Follow the path to a gate onto the road.

2. Turn right and go along the main road as far as a footpath and a sign for Richborough Roman Fort pointing right. Go along this quiet road with houses on one side and the Nature Reserve to the right. It continues after the houses as a country lane between high hedges. Just before the road bridge, follow the footpath sign to the right onto the river path.

3. This is the Saxon Shore Way. Keep right along the river, going through one gate until you reach a path junction. Where the Saxon Shore Way continues to follow the river, turn towards the railway and go over a stile to a railway crossing. Cross the railway and reach another stile.

4. Cross the stile and go left along a woodland path to the Roman fort. You will pass to the left of the Roman fort and get a good view of it. If you want to explore it further, there is a small museum and a charge to enter the grounds. Go straight on after the Roman fort, passing through the car park and taking the access road to reach the public road. There is a footpath but it is overgrown and best avoided.

5. Turn left on the road and follow it as it winds down to the railway. Cross at the level crossing and go under the road bridge to arrive back at the junction with the river path at point 3. As you continue along the road, look to the right to catch a glimpse of the White Mill windmill. It is open to the public and well worth a visit if you have time. Continue to retrace your outward path back to the car park.

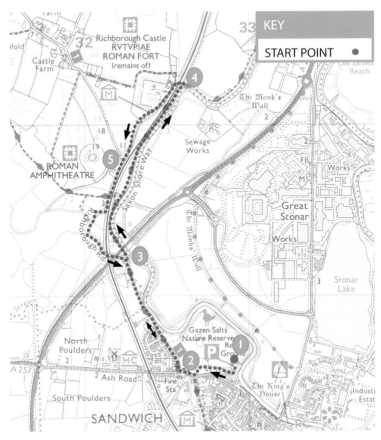

KEY

START POINT ●

DENTON

Visit the pub where scenes from the 1969 film *The Battle of Britain* were filmed and take a walk around this historic village.

The Jackdaw was built in 1645 as a farmhouse. It was not until 1756 that it became a public house, licensed to Andrew Snell, which he subsequently named the Red Lion. By the 19th century it was a coaching stop on the Canterbury to Folkestone road. The poet, Thomas Gray, the author of 'Elegy Written in a Country Churchyard', was a regular in the 18th century, as was Thomas Ingoldsby, the author of *The*

Ingoldsby Legends in the 19th century. Ingoldsby was the pen name of the clergyman Richard Harris Barham, who lived at nearby Tappington Hall, one of the oldest dwellings in Kent. His most famous tale was 'The Jackdaw of Rheims', from which the new name of the pub was derived. Although the pub has been altered and extended over the years, it still retains the character of the country inn, where scenes between Susannah York and Christopher Plummer for the 1969 movie were filmed. The rooms are filled with World War II and particularly RAF memorabilia, including model Spitfires and contemporary adverts.

The village is recorded in an Anglo-Saxon charter of 799 and in the Domesday Book of 1086 as Danetone, from the Old English *denu*, a valley, and *tun*, a settlement. Some of the houses, such as Lavender Cottage and Little Madekin are hundreds of years old and others such as the Old Bakery are reminders of a bygone time, when every small village in England had its own bakery.

The 13th-century St Mary Magdalene church, which you pass on the walk, still has fragments of 14th-century stained glass within. Next to the church is Denton Court, the site of the original manor house of the village, rebuilt in the 19th century by Sir Samuel Egerton Brydges. The best view of the house is as you descend the hill towards it, before you cross the road.

Edward Hasted, in his *History and Topographical Survey of the County of Kent* of 1800, described Denton as being in 'wild, dreary and mountainous country, the hills … rising on each side of the valley, pretty sudden and high'. He would not recognise it today. Many of the trees which covered the hills have gone, softening the landscape to pleasant, rolling meadows edged with woodland.

THE BASICS

Distance: 2 miles / 3.25km

Gradient: Gentle

Severity: Easy

Approx. time to walk: 1¼ hours

Stiles: Six

Map: OS Explorer 138 (Dover, Folkestone and Hythe)

Path description: Footpaths, fields and tracks

Start point: The Jackdaw. GR TR 215472

Parking: On 'The Street' Denton (CT4 6QZ) or at The Jackdaw (see below)

Dog friendly: No (stiles)

Toilets: No public toilets on the route

Nearest food: The Jackdaw serves some of the best food in Kent. There is a car park at the Jackdaw which you can use if you plan to patronise the pub but check with the landlord first.

DENTON WALK

1. With the Jackdaw behind you, carefully cross the road then bear left, up a lane following the sign pointing towards the village hall. At the end of the village hall, as the lane starts to turn left, turn right onto a footpath.

2. Head uphill on this towards a wood, keeping the fence to your right. When you reach the wood, bear left and enter the woods on a narrow, and possibly overgrown, footpath. Once through the first few feet it opens out to a lovely woodland walk. Keep going to reach a crossroads of paths with a way-marker post.

3. Turn left and head downhill to exit the wood. Keep ahead as you continue downhill over pastureland on a very narrow, but visible, path. After it passes the end of a banking on the left, the path bears slightly left to reach a junction with a lane and the road at the bottom.

4. Carefully cross the A260 and keep ahead, uphill on a dirt track. When you reach the edge of some trees, turn left and enter the churchyard through a gap in the fence. Pick your way through the gravestones to reach the church of St Mary Magdalene and have a look round inside. When you have finished leave the churchyard via the entrance gate and turn right. Keep an eye open on the way along this grassy path for a kissing gate in the metal fence to your right and turn towards it.

5. Go through the gate, cross a lane and pass through another kissing gate at the other side. Then keep going uphill until you intersect another path by a deep ditch. Cross the ditch and turn right, heading towards a stile which you cross, then cross

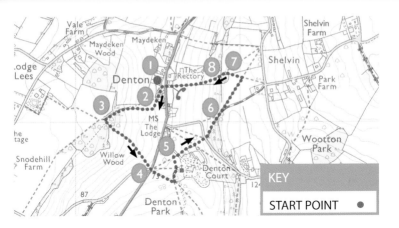

KEY

START POINT ●

a lane and take the public bridleway into the wood beyond. This heads uphill. When you reach a junction of paths keep left to exit the woods and go into a field.

6. Keep the line of the path to cross this pasture until you intersect another narrow footpath. Turn left onto it and head towards a wood. Enter this by a narrow path then cross a stile to exit it and turn left to follow the edge of the woods.

7. In the corner of the field cross another stile then take the path downhill through a wooded section and go over yet another stile, then through a gate to enter another field.

8. Follow the well-trodden path which curves left downhill, cross the stile in the corner and continue downhill through another field with the fence on your left. Finally go through a gate, cross a stile and go down some steps to enter the car park of the Jackdaw.

CAPEL-LE-FERNE

THE FRONTLINE OF THE BATTLE OF BRITAIN, A MEMORIAL TO 'THE FEW', REPLICA AIRCRAFT AND AN INTERACTIVE DISCOVERY CENTRE.

At the National Battle of Britain Memorial, the stone statue of a seated airman sits looking out from the White Cliffs towards the French coast. A pilot, sitting here in August 1940, would have seen German bombers with fighter escorts heading towards the coast to attack RAF airfields including nearby Hawkinge. The German strategy was to destroy British air defences prior to a full-scale invasion by sea and air.

On 10 July 1940 the Luftwaffe attacked shipping in the English Channel. They then escalated the campaign to attack major ports, RAF airfields and radar installations and bombed major industrial centres, targeting factories producing aircraft and armaments. In September they launched the Blitzkrieg, intensive attacks on major centres of population, particularly London, aimed at inflicting massive civilian casualties and undermining morale. Despite their efforts the resolve of the civilian population was actually strengthened by the attacks.

Losses of RAF aircraft and aircrew were considerable but a fraction of the losses of the Luftwaffe, who lacked the resources to provide sufficient replacements. In contrast, production and repairs in Britain kept pace with the losses and an intensive training programme was turning out replacement pilots at a rate that allowed Fighter Command to increase the number of pilots on frontline duty throughout the conflict. The Germans also made a series of tactical errors like stopping attacking radar stations, not realising that they were a vital part of the defence system.

The Germans launched two massive attacks on 15 September but the RAF took down sixty German aircraft, while losing twenty-six RAF planes. Two days later the invasion was shelved. Although the Battle of Britain is generally regarded as running from 10 July to 31 October 1940, it is 15 September that is commemorated as Battle of Britain Day. Victory was not cheap. Over 23,000 people died and 32,000 were wounded but it was the first defeat of Hitler's forces and a turning point in the war.

'Never in the field of human conflict was so much owed by so many to so few.' Churchill's famous words of the time are carved into a wall at the memorial. There is also a wall commemorating the names of 'The Few', along with replica Spitfire and Hurricane fighters and an interactive area with computers and archive footage.

THE BASICS

Distance: 2¼ miles / 3.6km

Gradient: One steep descent and climb

Severity: Moderate

Approx. time to walk: 1 hour

Stiles: None

Map: OS Explorer 138 (Dover, Folkestone and Hythe)

Path description: Coastal and field paths, some quite overgrown in summer. Long trousers and walking poles are recommended.

Start point: Car park at Battle of Britain Memorial (GR TR 244381)

Parking: Battle of Britain Memorial, New Dover Road (CT18 7JJ)

Dog friendly: Yes

Toilets: At Memorial

Nearest food: Café at Memorial

CAPEL-LE-FERNE WALK

1. From the car park head towards the  sea and join the coastal path. Go right on the path. There are short paths leading nearer to the cliff edge to appreciate the superb views. When you have had enough of the views continue on the broad grassy path. When you reach a fence, go through the gate onto a narrow path. Watch out for nettles in summer. At the end of the fence the path continues ahead but you are turning right alongside the fence.

2. The narrow path continues overgrown at parts, emerging at a busy road beside the Valiant Sailor pub. You need to cross the road here, but it is a very bad bend so go right a little way to the point opposite the footpath on the other side. Cross to the footpath and go on in the same direction. Shortly you will come to another short overgrown section, emerging onto a field.

3. Go right along the edge of the field until you reach a rough gravel road. Cross this and continue gently uphill alongside the hedge, then across a crop field. At the end of the crop field, take the narrow path ahead to reach a country lane.

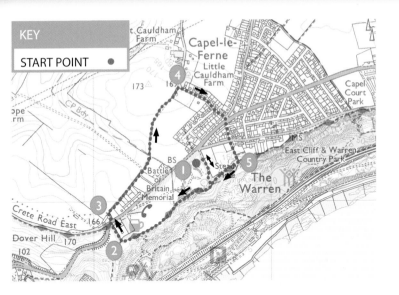

4. Go right on the lane to the main road. Look diagonally across the road to the right to see Capel Lane. Cross and go along it. Go to the right of the garage at the end and follow the lane. There is a public footpath stone marking it. Just before some houses, there are some stairs to the right.

5. Go down the stairs and up the other side to reach the coastal path and turn back towards the Memorial. When you get there take some time to look around before returning to the car park.

HAWKINGE

A FRONTLINE RAF AIRFIELD, A MAJOR FILM LOCATION AND
A MUSEUM THAT TELLS THE STORY OF THE BATTLE OF BRITAIN.

The Battle of Britain Museum occupies a small part of what was once RAF Hawkinge. As one of the nearest airfields to France it was in the front line for the Battle of Britain in an area that became notorious as 'Hellfire Corner'. Apart from the museum buildings the rest of the former airbase is now covered in modern housing. But before these were built it became an airfield one last time in the 1969 film *The Battle of Britain*.

This film set out to provide as accurate a portrayal as possible of the main events in the air battle. To help ensure historical accuracy the producers employed as consultants two of the most famous names from both sides of the conflict, Robert Stanford Tuck and Adolf Galland, and in an unusual departure from war films of the time they had German-speaking actors with subtitles.

The star-studded cast was headed by Laurence Olivier as Air Chief Marshal, Sir Hugh (Stuffy) Dowding, Trevor Howard played Sir Keith Park, officer in command of No. 11 Group and Patrick Wymark was Trafford Leigh-Mallory, commanding No. 12 Group. Christopher Plummer was cast as a Canadian pilot, Susannah York as his wife and Michael Caine as Squadron Leader Canfield. The cast also included Ralph Richardson, Ian McShane, Kenneth More, Michael Redgrave and Edward Fox. But the real stars of this film were the aircraft and in particular the Supermarine Spitfire and the Hawker Hurricane.

Most of the aircraft used for the flying scenes were on loan but the museum houses some full-size replicas of both aircraft and three full-size replica Messerschmitts, which were used in the film. There's also a collection of Rolls-Royce Merlin engines, which were used to power both Spitfires and Hurricanes.

The film concentrates on the conflict between Park and Leigh-Mallory over the proposed 'Big Wings' where several squadrons would join up in the air to attack the enemy. In theory this would result in greater enemy losses but they were slow to form up and time on the ground refuelling made them more vulnerable to attack. Dowding supported Park's opposition to 'Big Wings' and hindsight has proved them to be right. Nevertheless, despite his role in winning the Battle of Britain, when it was over Dowding was sacked.

THE BASICS

Distance: 2 miles / 3.2km

Gradient: Flat

Severity: Easy

Approx. time to walk: 1 hour

Stiles: None

Map: OS Explorer 138 (Dover, Folkestone and Hythe)

Path description: Road, field paths and country lanes. Long trousers and walking sticks are recommended to deal with nettles.

Start point: Kent Battle of Britain Museum (TR 207395)

Parking: Battle of Britain Museum, Aerodrome Road (CT18 7AG)

Dog friendly: Yes, but keep on a lead in cemetery

Toilets: Cemetery

Nearest food: Pubs in Hawkinge

HAWKINGE WALK

1. From the museum turn right along Aerodrome Road. Look on the right for a memorial to the airfield and its personnel. Continue to the roundabout and go around and have a look at the bunker before going on across the roundabout towards the cemetery.

2. Turn left into the cemetery and then take the first path to the right to the graves of the German airmen. Pass these and go on towards the large cross to find the British graves. Look at the last row to find the graves of those who died in the Battle of Britain, poignantly British and German together. Walk along the path behind the graves to re-join the main path through the cemetery. Turn right towards the chapel. Go left through the car park and pass to the left of the chapel and along a small path along the edge of the cemetery. When the path bends to the right, go left through a gap in the hedge into a field.

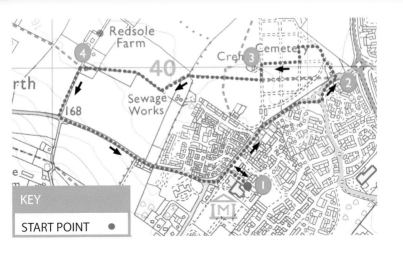

KEY

START POINT ●

3. Go left along the edge of the field and continue in the same direction across to a hedge. Look for an opening in the hedge, quite overgrown in summer but easily passable. Emerge into a field and follow the clear path across the crop field to a farm track, which leads to a country lane.

4. Turn left onto the lane and continue to a T-junction and turn left. This is the other end of Aerodrome Road, which leads all the way back to the museum.

ELHAM

This picturesque village has witty 19th-century stained glass and more than its fair share of famous former residents from prime minister Anthony Eden to a young Audrey Hepburn and the proponent of the famous 'Parkinson's Law'.

The village is listed in the Domesday Book of 1086 as Alham but it was settled long before that. Hundreds of Neolithic tools and some Bronze Age remains have been found. The church of St Mary, which is in the square at the start of the walk, is 12th or 13th century and some 13th-century windows remain. However, the most interesting windows are the 19th-century work of the vicar of the time, Walter Wodehouse, and his brother and sister. A young David is portrayed, with the face of Madame Patti, a famous singer of the day, playing the harp. On the next window Saul, with the face of Thomas Carlyle, is seated on his throne, while behind the throne are the two most famous prime ministers of the age, Disraeli and Gladstone. The prime minister of the day, Lord Salisbury, is depicted behind David as Samuel. On a window alongside this, Walter Wodehouse himself is depicted as David on his throne as an old man.

Opposite the church look for a house called Five Bells. This cottage, then called Orchard Cottage, was where Audrey Hepburn lived from 1935 to 1940. She went to school at a small private school in the village square, run by the Misses Rigden, and left to fly to Holland on her 11th birthday.

Sir Anthony Eden, British prime minister from 1955 to 1957, lived at Park Gate House, just outside the village, during World War II, when he was Foreign Secretary. He was visited there, on more than one occasion, by Winston Churchill.

At Elham Manor House on the Old Road at the top of Culling's Hill, Professor Cyril Northcote Parkinson lived for a time. He was a writer, historian and university professor, but his main claim to fame is Parkinson's Law: that work expands to fill the time available. He originally proposed the idea in a witty article for the London *Economist*, in 1955 and then included it in his book, ***Parkinson's Law: The Pursuit of Progress***, published in 1957. It was a great insight at the time and is probably even more true today, when too much information can make the simplest task complex.

THE BASICS

Distance: 2½ miles / 4km

Gradient: Negligible

Severity: Easy

Approx. time to walk: 1¼ hours

Stiles: None

Map: OS Explorer 138 (Dover, Folkestone and Hythe)

Path description: Pavement, lanes and footpaths

Start point: The Square, Elham (GR TR 177438)

Parking: The Square (CT4 6TJ) (free but limited spaces)

Dog friendly: Yes

Toilets: High Street

Nearest food: The King's Arms at the start of the walk or the Cosy Tea Rooms on the High Street

ELHAM WALK

1. From The Square head away from the King's Arms and turn left into Duck Street. Then turn right to enter the churchyard of St Mary the Virgin. After you have visited the church and explored the churchyard exit via the same gate and continue down Duck Street. The house on your left with the impressive garden is Five Bells. This was where a young girl called Audrey Ruston, later Hepburn, and her mother lived for a while with Mr and Mrs Butcher.

2. Just past the end of the 30 mph zone turn left at a footpath sign onto the Elham Valley Way. Continue on a footpath by the edge of fields and keep on it as it turns right then, when it ends, go through a kissing gate and follow the path by the hedge to reach another kissing gate that leads onto a lane.

3. Turn left along the lane then, after passing buildings on both sides of the road turn left at a footpath sign and go along a track, go through a gate and continue past farm buildings to go through another kissing gate into a pasture and keep ahead on a narrow footpath. Go through two more kissing gates, keeping ahead, then after the next gate veer right across a field following a narrow, but visible path. Go through a gate at the end of the field and along a wide grassy track to reach a T-junction.

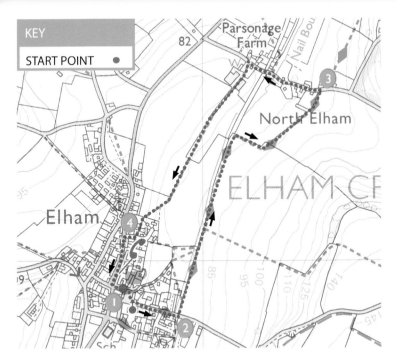

KEY

START POINT ●

4. Turn right into Cherry Gardens and at the next T-junction go left into High Street and head downhill. Pass Lime Villas on your left and the Baptist Church on your right. At the bottom of the street the Cosy Tea Rooms and the Abbot's Fireside are on the right and the Rose and Crown on the left. Turn left after the Rose and Crown into St Mary's Road and go along it to return to the Square.

ENJOY A BEAUTIFUL BEACH WALK FOLLOWED BY A STROLL
ALONG THE TOWPATH OF A CANAL WITH A DIFFERENCE.

The walk starts along a lovely pebble beach. The water quality here is excellent and the beach is cleaned daily. On a clear day you can see the coast of France, which is only 23 miles (37km) away. At the beginning of the 19th century, Napoleon Bonaparte was openly planning an invasion of England, having said, 'All my thoughts are directed towards England. I want only for a favourable wind to plant the Imperial Eagle on the Tower of London.'

When you leave the beach, you turn onto the Royal Military Canal. This was built in response to the threat from Napoleon, starting in 1804. It is 28 miles (45km) long and extends in an arc around Romney Marsh from Hythe to Cliff End in Sussex. The canal was built with kinks in it every 600 yards for gun emplacements to allow them to cover the length of the canal against invaders. Behind the canal was a rampart and behind that a military road to enable swift movement of troops and supplies. By the time the canal was completed in 1809, the threat of invasion had disappeared after the French naval defeat at Trafalgar in 1805 and so the canal was regarded as a huge waste of public money.

To try to recoup some of the costs the government opened the canal to trade and levied tolls but it never paid its way and as the railway system grew throughout the 19th century,

the canal declined, as did the whole canal network, even those built on obvious trade routes. Nowadays the canal is used for leisure. You will see fishers at intervals along its banks and you can hire a boat to spend a pleasant hour or two on the water.

The town of Hythe was always regarded as a significant defensive point. It was one of the Cinque Ports, which enjoyed privileges in return for providing ships for the sovereign when necessary. Although Hythe remains on the sea, unlike some of the other Cinque Ports, its harbour has silted up to the point that there is now no trace of it left. Several of the Martello Towers, built in the early 19th century as defences against Napoleon, were sited along the coast at Hythe. Look out for the remains of some of these as you leave Hythe.

THE BASICS

Distance: 4¾ miles / 7.6km
Gradient: Flat
Severity: Easy
Approx. time to walk: 2 hours
Stiles: None
Map: OS Explorer 138 (Dover, Folkestone and Hythe)
Path description: Promenade, canal path and footpaths
Start point: Twiss Road (GR TR 168343)
Parking: Twiss Road car park (CT21 6AE)
Dog friendly: Yes
Toilets: On route, in park
Nearest food: Hythe High Street is just off the walk and has many outlets

HYTHE WALK

1. Leave the car park and head east along the promenade (parallel with Princess Parade) with the sea on your right. Or, if you feel inclined, go onto the shingle beach and walk along it. Pass a National Cycle Network Millennium Mile marker showing 4 miles to Folkestone.

2. After approximately a mile and a half (2km) leave the promenade and cross the road to enter the car park at the Royal Military Canal. Keep ahead to the interpretation boards then turn left to go down some steps to the canal. Turn right and walk a short distance to see the pool at the end of the canal.

3. Return to the foot of the steps and continue to walk ahead along the grassy path by the side of the canal. Walk past three footbridges. The golf course will be on your left after the third. At the end of the golf course keep on the path to reach a road bridge.

4. Carefully cross the road then turn right over the bridge and left back onto the canal and bear right to take the path along the banking that runs beside the canal. Pass another footbridge beside a war memorial.

5. Just after the memorial look up to your right to see the 11th-century St Leonard's Church up on the hill. It has a collection of 2,000 skulls and 8,000 thigh bones in the crypt, which you can visit for a very modest charge. The path then joins Rampart Road. If you want to explore the historic town centre cross the road at the pedestrian lights and head up to the High Street.

6. Otherwise turn left to cross the bridge at Stade Street then left again onto the opposite bank of the canal. To your left just past another millennium mile marker is a seed dispenser where you can buy food to feed the ducks. In another short distance there's a rowing boat hire centre that operates from Easter to September.

7. Then turn right onto Ladies Walk, take the first left onto the Wakefield Walk, pass tennis courts on your right and keep on to the end of the path.

8. Exit onto the main road opposite Moncreiff Gardens and turn right. Follow this road back to the car park.

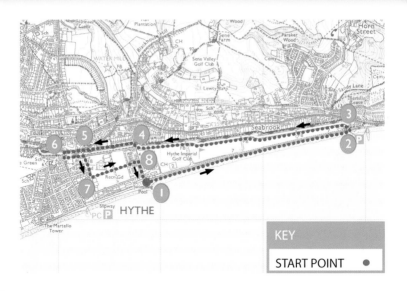

OLD ROMNEY

TALES OF SMUGGLERS, MEDIEVAL CHURCHES, A FAMOUS FILM DIRECTOR AND WALT DISNEY. WHAT MORE COULD YOU ASK FOR ON A WALK?

In the 18th century Kent was a hotbed of smugglers. The smuggling started when the export of wool was banned and fleeces were smuggled across the Channel. This ended when the French realised they could get cheaper wool from Ireland. However, the smuggling of brandy, tobacco, tea and silk from France continued. Tea in particular was heavily taxed in England, at 119 per cent, while there was almost no taxation on the Continent. Needless to say most of the tea consumed in England was smuggled.

There were several famous smuggling gangs in Kent, most notably the Hawkhurst Gang, who took their name from the village just ten miles north of Romney Marsh and had reputedly around five hundred members. Any opposition to them, be it rival gangs or excise men, was dealt with violently.

However, the most famous smuggling gang in the area did not actually exist. It was led by the fictitious Dr Syn, who was the hero of a series of novels by Russell Thorndyke. By day he was the respectable vicar of St Peter and Paul in Dymchurch but by night he was the Scarecrow, the leader of the local smugglers. Local clergy were commonly complicit in smuggling activities in return for 'brandy for the parson, baccy for the clerk' but it is unlikely that any were as heavily involved as Thorndyke's character.

When the Walt Disney Company made a film series featuring Dr Syn in 1962, the church at Dymchurch had been greatly altered, so they used St Clement's instead. It's one of the oldest churches in Kent with most of the building dating from the 12th century. The 18th-century box pews were painted pink for the filming and the congregation liked them so much they have kept them that way. In the churchyard is the grave of the famous film director Derek Jarman.

The other medieval church on this walk, St George's at Ivychurch, is larger than you would expect because it was built under the patronage of the Archbishop of Canterbury. Legend has it that there were times when it was impossible to have a service there because of the contraband being stored. Next door the Bell Inn was a famous smugglers' pub and there are supposed to be tunnels linking it to the church.

THE BASICS

Distance: 5 miles / 8km

Gradient: Flat

Severity: Easy

Approx. time to walk: 2½ hours

Stiles: None

Map: OS Explorer 125 (Romney Marsh)

Path description: Country lanes, B road and footpaths (some rather overgrown)

Start point: St Clement's Church (GR TR 034252)

Parking: St Clements Church, Old Romney (TN29 0HP)

Dog friendly: Yes

Toilets: None on route

Nearest food: The Bell in Ivychurch

OLD ROMNEY WALK

1. Walk back along the road from the church and keep ahead at the junction. As you approach the first bend on this road look for a footpath marker on your left. This is a footpath that will take you round a moat but it's quite overgrown so you may decide to continue along the lane. At the next bend the footpath rejoins the road at another way-marker.

2. From the lane turn left and then take the faint footpath that runs on the left side of a drainage ditch. Follow this as it curves round to the left then turns right and then left.

3. As it crosses a broad track keep ahead to cross a footbridge then continue in the same direction to reach another crossroads with a broad, but overgrown, track. This is Yoakes Lane.

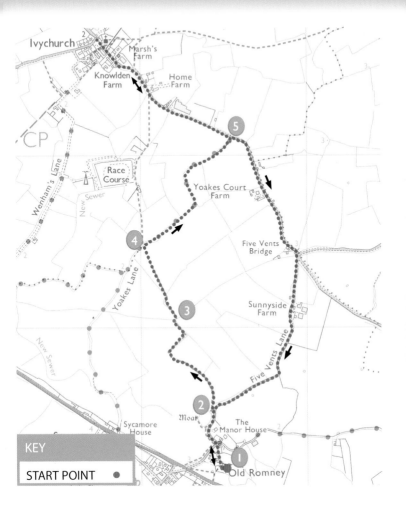

4.   Turn right onto it and follow it for some distance until it reaches the main road.

5.   Turn left and follow the road into the village of Ivychurch. Visit the churchyard and church and if you require refreshments, the Bell Inn next door to the church. Then go back along the road in the opposite direction. Pass Yoakes Court farm and Five Vents Bridge to reach a road junction.

6.   Turn right onto Five Vents Lane and follow it past Sunnyside Farm and then the moat, to return to the start.

FAIRFIELD

MEDIEVAL CHURCHES, VANISHED VILLAGES AND THE RECLAIMED LAND BETWEEN THE OLD SHORELINE AND THE ENGLISH CHANNEL.

Romney Marsh is a fascinating place where agricultural land has been reclaimed from the sea. It's a maze of watery ditches, criss-crossed by narrow lanes with anonymous junctions with no signposts. While it is famous for its emptiness it is nevertheless one of the most attractive corners of Kent and has been an inspiration to writers, artists and poets.

A very young Noel Coward took up residence in a cottage next door to the 15th-century Star Inn in St Mary in The Marsh. It is directly opposite the medieval church of St Mary the Virgin where you will find the simple wooden grave marker of Edith Nesbit, author of *The Railway Children*, who spent the last few years of her life in a house in St Mary's Bay. She and Coward became friends and he would later write that the secret of her success was 'her extraordinary power of describing hot summer days in England in the beginning years of the century'.

In all there were twelve medieval churches in the marshes, built by lords of the various manors. Two of the twelve are on the Old Romney walk. The one on this walk is the most photographed of them all, St Thomas à Becket at Fairfield. In 2011 it was used as a location in the BBC production of Dickens's *Great Expectations* starring David Suchet and a film of the same title with Helena Bonham Carter and Ralph Fiennes.

The church stands in splendid isolation on top of an artificial mound, surrounded by sheep grazed pasture and watery dykes. Originally a timber-framed, wattle and daub construction, the frame was replaced in the 15th century and the wattle and daub gave way to bricks in the 18th. Near to collapse it was totally rebuilt in 1912 but most of the original building material was re-used. The causeway was built then so the builders could access the site but even then it was often surrounded by water and worshippers had to be ferried over in boats. The interior is spectacular with 18th-century white box pews, a triple-decker pulpit and ancient woodwork.

Other churches have vanished for a variety of reasons. Some succumbed to storms in the 13th and 14th centuries, while others lost their congregations to the Black Death or malaria.

THE BASICS

Distance: 2 miles / 3.2km
Gradient: Flat
Severity: Easy
Approx. time to walk: 1 hour
Stiles: None
Map: OS Explorer 125 (Romney Marsh)
Path description: Country lane and field
Start point: Lay-by near Fairfield Church (GR TQ 966264)
Parking: Lay-by next to the church (TN29 9RZ)
Dog friendly: Yes
Toilets: None on walk
Nearest food: Pub at Brookland

FAIRFIELD WALK

1. From the lay-by turn left and head along the lane to pass Becket Barn Farm. As you pass by, look to your left and beside the garage door you will see where to get the church key later.

2. Turn left just past here at a finger post and head along a broad, well-surfaced track. Keep on this to the gate just before the house, Beckets Court then turn left, through a gate.

3. There is no footpath sign, way-marker or even a faint track to guide you but take a line about forty-five degrees from the gate and head across the field, making towards a gate and beyond it a bridge. At the time of writing there was an electric fence across the field. This may be temporary but if it is still there turn right along it to reach the end near the drainage dyke then cross it. Follow the dyke to reach the gate. Go through it and cross the bridge.

4. The path now veers slightly right. If the field is in crop there should be a clearly visible path to follow. Otherwise head towards the only house you can see in that direction. Go through a kissing gate then keep on the same line through crops to reach another kissing gate by a finger post.

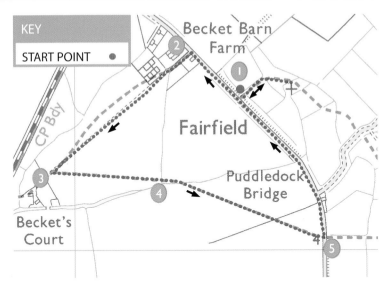

KEY

START POINT ●

Becket Barn Farm

Fairfield

Puddledock Bridge

Becket's Court

CP Bdy

5. Go through this then turn left onto a lane. Follow this past a junction on your right to return to your vehicle. Then turn right to go through the gate and follow the path along the causeway to visit the church. If you want to see the interior then return to Becket Barn Farm to collect the key. Do not take it as you pass earlier on the walk as you will be depriving other visitors of the opportunity to see inside. And don't forget to return the key when you are finished.

SISSINGHURST

AFTER A LOVELY WALK THROUGH THE ESTATE, SPEND SOME TIME EXPLORING THE INCOMPARABLE GARDENS OF SISSINGHURST.

The castle at Sissinghurst was built in the 16th century, by generations of the Baker family. By the end of the century it was a grand house around a massive courtyard, fronted by the magnificent twin-towered gateway that remains today. However, by the 17th century the house was in decline. It suffered severe damage from its use as a prisoner-of-war camp and despite new building and improvements by Victorian owners, the Mann Cornwallis family, the house never really recovered. By the time Vita Sackville-West and her husband Harold Nicolson came to buy it in 1930, the original tower and buildings were in a state of ruin.

Both Vita and Harold contributed to the creation of the garden, with his designs and her exuberant planting, although sometimes she would choose simplicity while he opted for showy extravagance. The garden was made fairly quickly and was opened to the public for the first time in 1937. The walk takes you by the moat and the gazebo, through wild flower meadows, past the vegetable garden and through the new orchard, giving an idea of the extent of the estate. If you visit the garden, first climb the tower to get an overview.

The gardens have been designed in harmony with the buildings so that the warm brick of house and walls are draped with flowers and greenery, through which peep the leaded panes of the windows. Each garden is separate, so as you walk through an arch or a hedge you will find a riot of red and yellow in the cottage garden, the breath-taking shades of white and cream in the white garden, the blues, reds and violets of the purple border or the calm ordered walks between hedges or alongside the moat.

Vita and Harold always had gardeners, in particular, Jack Vass, head gardener from 1939 to 1957, of whom Vita wrote, 'let Vass live strong and healthy until he is eighty at least, and never let him be tempted away to anyone else's garden.' Vita died in 1962 and, to avoid death duties, the estate came into the ownership of the National Trust in  1967. Over the years, the head gardeners of Sissinghurst have managed the delicate balance of maintaining the garden created by Vita and Harold, while making subtle changes as plants grow or die.

THE BASICS

Distance: 3½ miles / 5.6km

Gradient: Slight

Severity: Easy

Approx. time to walk: 1½ hours

Stiles: Two

Map: OS Explorer 137 (Ashford)

Path description: Estate paths

Start point: The car park at Sissinghurst (GR TQ 805383)

Parking: Sissinghurst car park (TN17 2AB) (normal National trust charges apply)

Dog friendly: Yes, if they can manage stiles

Toilets: At Sissinghurst

Nearest food: Cafe at Sissinghurst

SISSINGHURST WALK

1. Leave the car park and turn left into the estate grounds. Turn right in front of the garden shop and follow the lane towards the house. Pass the oast houses on your left, turn left then fork right just before the building with the arch. You are now on a track that skirts round the side of the gardens. Keep on it until it terminates at a T-junction onto a lane.

2. Turn left onto the lane and follow it until it bends left and enters woodland. When you reach a track road junction turn left onto a bridleway.

3. This goes past a cottage on the left and emerges into a pasture. Keep ahead across this then continue along a long, shady, hedge-lined tunnel. When this ends at a junction turn left, cross the lane and enter the orchard.

4. Veer left across this and at the other end go through a gate and continue for a short distance along a hedge.

5. Then turn left through another gate and head downhill, through pastureland, with a hedge on your left. Then go through a gate, turn left onto a path and follow it to pass by a gate and exit onto a lane.

6. Turn left then almost immediately right across a collapsing stile before turning left and walking along a meadow by a hedge. Near the end of this, turn left across a similar stile, turn right onto the lane and then left to return to the car park.

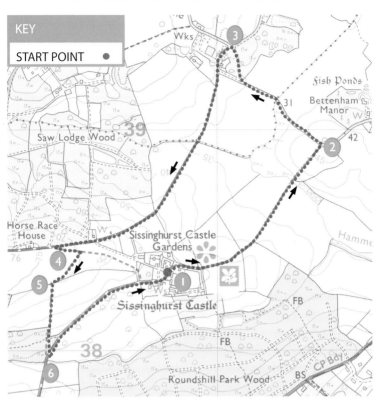

KEY

START POINT ●

ABOUT THE AUTHORS

Moira McCrossan and Hugh Taylor are a husband and wife writing team now specialising in travel for the over 50's and walking guides. They are also travel editors of the UK's premier over 50's web site laterlife.com.

Moira McCrossan spent most of her working life in education and was a Primary School Head Teacher. An active trade unionist she is a former President of the Educational Institute of Scotland, served on the general council of the Scottish TUC and the executive committee of the Women's National Commission for whom she co-authored the report, Growing up Female in the UK. She was also a frequent contributor to the Times Educational Supplement (Scotland).

Hugh Taylor is an Award winning travel writer, broadcaster and photographer. He worked extensively for BBC Radio, producing several series for Radio 2 including Doomsday in the Afternoon about the music of the Scottish Travellers.

Together they have written or contributed to over forty travel and outdoor guides, some of which have been translated into several languages. They range from major country guides covering Scotland, Lebanon and Jordan to walking books throughout the UK. Their work has appeared worldwide in publications as diverse as The Times, Women's Realm, Choice, The Herald, Interval World and the Glencairn Gazette. They live in the picturesque southern Scottish village of Moniaive (www.moniaive.org.uk).

Acknowledgements

The authors would like to thank Rob Ganley, Andrew Robson and The Camping and Caravanning Club for providing us with a base from which to do the walks and the research for this book; the Managers and Assistant Managers at Oldbury, Canterbury and Norman's Bay Camping and Caravanning Club Sites for help and advice; and Alan Macfadyen for walk suggestions and for sharing his comprehensive historical knowledge of the area.